THE GOLDEN YEAR

BY RENA KORB
ILLUSTRATED BY ERIC REECE

PEARSON

Scott
Foresman

Editorial Offices: Glenview, Illinois • Parsippany, New Jersey • New York, New York
Sales Offices: Needham, Massachusetts • Duluth, Georgia • Glenview, Illinois
Coppell, Texas • Ontario, California • Mesa, Arizona

ISBN: 0-328-13584-4

4 5 6 7 8 9 10 V0G1 14 13 12 11 10 09 08 07 06

CONTENTS:

CHAPTER 1:
GETTING READY TO GO

January 16, 1849: Pa came home with news today. He said we are going to move to California. He said gold is everywhere, even in the streets! Ten-year-old boys like me can dig for gold. I think it sounds like a grand adventure, but Ma and Susannah looked a little scared. This means we are probably leaving Macon, Missouri, forever.

Since Pa's big announcement, the whole family had been hard at work. Ma and Pa sold the farm and nearly all our possessions. Ma shed more than a few tears as she gathered her pewter bowls and plates to sell. They wouldn't fit in the wagon. Susannah joined in shedding tears as she had to decide which of her dolls to leave behind.

Joshua didn't feel bad about leaving most of his possessions behind. His favorite things are small enough to fit in his pocket—a marble and a slingshot Pa had carved out of wood.

It was now time to leave. From the back of the wagon, Joshua watched as the only home he had ever known faded farther and farther away into the distance.

First, Joshua and his family had to make their way to Independence, Missouri, before setting out on the California Trail, across the unknown landscape of the vast Great Plains. Joshua helped Pa prepare for their journey. At the store, they bought warm clothes, sturdy boots, and needles and thread. They selected barrels for storing water, an iron cookstove, tin plates and cups, tools, a canvas tent, and even a spare wagon wheel. They bought bacon, ham, and bags of rice, dried fruit, tea, coffee, and flour.

"I can't wait to get started, Pa," Josh said one afternoon. "This is going to be the best trip ever."

"I hope so," said Pa. "You know, Joshua," he said slowly, "at times, this journey is going to be very difficult." That night, the family warmed themselves by the fire long after dinner was done.

"Pa, will you tell us about the Great Plains?" asked Susannah.

So, Pa told stories about the buffalo stampeding across the broad prairies. Susannah and Joshua listened excitedly. "The Great Plains lie before us for miles, empty except for buffalo, jackrabbits, Indians, and our little wagon train. Now off to sleep, you two."

At Independence, Pa joined several other gold-seekers who were making the overland journey. Ten or so wagons had decided to travel together. "It will be easier that way," Pa said. But Joshua knew that Pa also thought that traveling with more people would make the trip safer.

Whatever the reason for the wagon train, Joshua was happy with the plan. He had just met the Krupps, a family from Germany, who were part of the group. Their son Hermann was about Joshua's age. At first, Joshua found it difficult to communicate with Hermann. The German boy had recently arrived in America and spoke little English. But when the boys weren't helping their fathers, and when Joshua wasn't minding Susannah, the two boys explored the town of Independence. Even if they didn't have long talks, Joshua liked having a friend again.

Joshua spent most of his time assisting Pa. One of the most important jobs was packing their covered wagon. It stretched nine feet long and five feet wide. When Joshua had first looked inside the empty wagon, it had seemed huge. Now that everything the family owned had to fit inside the wagon, Joshua wasn't so sure.

CHAPTER 2:
LIFE ON THE TRAIL

May 12, 1849: Tomorrow is the big day. We're all packed up and ready. We have to get up really early and take the wagons out on the trail. I just know this is going to be the best adventure of my whole life.

Finally, the day came. The wagon train was ready to go. The sun had hardly risen in the sky when the line of wagons slowly pulled away from the town of Independence. Susannah sat up on the wagon's seat with Ma, who was holding the reins. Joshua walked with Pa next to the oxen that hauled the wagon. "If I'm not in the wagon, the oxen won't get as tired," Josh explained to Ma.

As he walked, Joshua observed his surroundings. He could see the long line of wagons making slow progress before him. The prairie seemed to stretch endlessly in every direction. It looked like a realm of enchantment. The tall prairie grass waved in the breeze and rustled as a rabbit or a prairie chicken ran through it. Wildflowers poked their heads above the grass. Above them, not a cloud dotted the bright, blue sky.

When the wagon halted, and Ma and Pa could switch off handling the reins, Susannah jumped down from her perch. "I want to pick some flowers for you, Ma," she said. She and Joshua ran across the prairie, picking flowers and reveling in the warmth of the sun on their faces. When Susannah gave the flowers to Ma, Ma smiled and tucked them into her bonnet. "Thank you, Susannah," she said.

"Pa, we must have gone ten miles," said Joshua as the sun sank lower in the sky.

"More than that, Joshua," Pa said. "I'd say we'll have gone at least fifteen before we make camp."

Just before sunset, the wagon train came to a halt. The wagons formed a tight circle with the travelers in the middle. Next to their wagon, Pa and Joshua pitched the tent, while Ma and Susannah helped build a fire and prepared dinner. Then they all gathered around and had their first dinner on the prairie.

Before turning in that night, many of the pioneers gathered around the central campfire. Together, they sang about the promised land ahead.

*We've formed our band and we're all
    well-manned
To journey afore to the promised land,
Where the golden ore is rich in store,
On the banks of Sacramento shore.
Then, ho! Boys ho! To California go.
There's plenty of gold in the world we're told
On the banks of the Sacramento!*

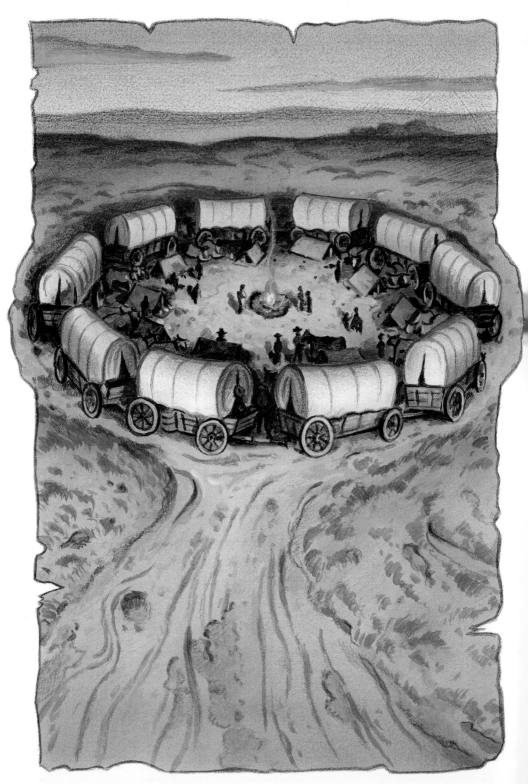

That night, Joshua barely got any sleep. At first, he couldn't help but stare up at the dazzling stars. The Milky Way cut a shimmering path through the night sky. When he closed his eyes, he dreamed of a buffalo stampede and thought he heard the calls of coyotes and the snuffling sounds of prowling bears.

Joshua and Hermann spent long afternoons making up games so that the time would pass more quickly. They scampered next to the wagon train, pretending to be a variety of animals. Hermann, slithering along on his belly through the tall grass, was a snake. Joshua put his hands to his forehead, made horns with his fingers, and charged toward Hermann like a buffalo.

Poor Susannah didn't have anyone her age to play with. She sat in the wagon, a doll in each hand, pretending they were her friends from back in Macon. One day, Susannah didn't want to play with her dolls. "I'm tired of this," she announced.

"Hop on down and explore with your brother," Ma suggested. "Don't wander too far from the wagons, though."

Joshua clasped Susannah's hand. At first, they trailed along behind the wagons, but then Susannah saw a small critter in the grass. "Let's follow it," she pleaded. "Oh, please, Joshua, please." So they bounded after it. Soon the wagon train was so far behind them that they couldn't see it.

Joshua, Hermann, and Susannah didn't notice how far they had wandered off. They stumbled into a clearing with a stream. As the stream moved, it got bigger and faster. They kept following the stream, until it plunged off a high cliff. Joshua and Susannah ran to the edge of the rock and looked over. The water from the stream struck the rocks below with such a force! It sent up a spray that cooled their faces.

Their adventure came to a quick end as Pa and Mr. Krupps charged up. "Where have you been? We had to ask other travelers to help us search for you! Your ma was afraid you'd be eaten by wolves."

"I'm sorry, Pa," Joshua said, hanging his head. "I'll be more careful in the future, I promise."

CHAPTER 3:
PROBLEMS ON THE PLAINS

July 3, 1849: The grown-ups seem to be getting more anxious the farther we travel from Missouri. They miss their homes, is what they say. The land is changing too. The prairie looks empty. There aren't any trees, and the grass is low and dry. It's hard to believe that anyone, even the Indians, can live out here.

Soon, problems started. First, a terrible hailstorm rained down on the wagon train. To Joshua, the hailstones looked as big as fists. The wagons had to stop and the travelers lost precious time. Pa looked nervous because he knew that they had to reach California before winter came and snow fell on the Sierra Nevada.

When the wagons were able to move again, the rain and melting hail had turned the trail into a muddy track. Every step from the team of oxen was a struggle. Then the wagons reached one of the broad rivers that criss-cross the Plains. A calmly flowing river would have provided much-needed drinking water for people and animals. Only this river was swollen and raging. Several of the men gathered on the bank to see how fast and how deep the water was.

The men decided the group needed to proceed. One by one, the wagons slowly picked their way across the river, with the women and children in the back of the wagons, and the men sitting up front and guiding the oxen. One by one, each family gathered on the opposite shore and watched the people still to come. Finally, the last wagon, with a hog tied to its back, was making the crossing. A gush of water roared down the river, and the hog disappeared. When the wagon finally made it to dry land, the woman inside could no longer hold back her tears. Her husband put his arm around her shoulders. "At least it was only the pig," he said.

Within a week following the harrowing river crossing, the Plains had totally changed. All the water and mud had dried up. The surface of the Plains had baked into hard, lifeless clay.

The band of pioneers marched along for days. Joshua and Hermann even grew tired of chasing each other, which had been their favorite game. Then something happened that provided a breathtaking change of pace, if only for a short time.

It started with a slight tremble. Then the ground began shaking. Within a few minutes, Joshua could hear a steady thumping sound. His whole body was vibrating.

"What is it, Pa?" he called. Pa held up a hand. He jumped down from the wagon and placed his ear against the hard ground. Then he called for the wagons to stop.

As the noise grew louder than thunder, a herd of buffalo charged past them. Joshua felt as if a dream had come true. Though the animals moved swiftly, Joshua could see their dark brown fur, their horns, and some young calves. Joshua was spellbound by these enormous, swift beasts.

Soon after, the trail began to climb up toward the South Pass. It was a slow, steady ascent. When they reached the top of the South Pass, they were at the Continental Divide, atop the Rocky Mountains. They were halfway to California.

The families now prepared to face the desert that spread out between them and the Sierra Nevada. At a clear stream, they filled their water barrels. When the travelers reached the desert, nothing seemed to be alive except for a few circling buzzards.

On their second day in the desert, Joshua heard water bubbling softly. Before them was a hot spring with water boiling to the surface. The water looked good, but it smelled like rotten eggs. A few of the travelers rushed forward to sample the spring. "Wait!" cried Mr. Krupps. "Don't drink it! This water will make you sick." Most people listened; the few who didn't got stomachaches.

After many days in the desert, the travelers walked down a gently sloping ridge. To their delight, they saw a grove of trees ahead. They had made it!

After leaving the desert, the travelers rested for a day. They knew that ahead of them loomed the hardest part of all. They had to cross mountains—the dreaded Sierra Nevada—before the snow started to fall. As they climbed higher into the mountains, it got much colder. The campfires burned only dimly, barely able to chase away the frigid night air. Susannah shivered while she slept. The next night, Ma pulled Pa aside for a talk. In an instant after their conversation, Pa chopped up Ma's favorite chair and threw it on the fire. The blaze shot up, and Susannah and Joshua inched closer to the flame. Joshua looked at his mother as she watched a piece of her family history go up in smoke. She didn't look sad, just determined.

A few days later, the mountain trail got steeper. The oxen could not pull their wagons any farther. The men unhitched them and roped them together in one long chain. Then they hitched the oxen to Mr. Krupp's wagon. The animals struggled to pull the wagon up the mountain. Once they reached the top, the men unhitched the team and led them back down for the next wagon. All the wagons were finally pulled to the top of the ridge.

CHAPTER 4:
WELCOME TO CALIFORNIA

October 10, 1849: Finally we have arrived in California. After making our way down the western slopes of the Sierra, we crossed the Sacramento Valley and arrived in San Francisco. Ma said if she couldn't have a hot bath and a new dress, we might as well just leave her in the Sierra. Pa said going to San Francisco was a good idea anyway. We could pick up supplies and trade our oxen for horses before heading back to the foothills to pan for gold and make our fortune. Hermann and his family headed straight out to the diggings. I hope we'll see them again.

Joshua walked around the bustling city of San Francisco in a daze. To his surprise, the streets were not paved with gold. Still, it was thrilling to see tall buildings, stores and theaters, and signs in many different languages lining the streets. "Look! Look!" Joshua and Susannah called out, tugging at each other's arms to point out another fascinating sight.

If the sights of San Francisco did not overwhelm Joshua, the steady noise did. Newsboys cried out the headlines at every corner, and storekeepers stood in front of their shops and called out their goods. Music tumbled out of the doors of a cafe.

Joshua's family stayed in San Francisco for only a few days. It was too expensive. Their room in the boarding house cost ten times as much as it would have back home. "My word!" Ma said when she found out that one apple cost ten cents. After buying supplies, the family packed up their wagon and headed for the land called Gold Mountain.

At the foot of the hills, they passed new arrivals buying supplies. These gold-seekers looked weary and dusty. For a while, their wagon rattled through empty, grass-covered land. "This is beautiful," Ma said softly.

Then they rode into the Pleasant Valley Gold Mines that Pa had read about in the guide book. "Looks like a lot of other people read the same book," Ma said, as they saw the main street lined with tents.

When Pa returned, he had a smile on his face. "Pleasant Valley has been mined out. I've learned there is gold just a ways from here at Weaverville," Pa said.

The next morning, Ma fried up a few slabs of bacon and served biscuits sweetened with sugar because it was a special day. Then Pa took Joshua with him on his search for a claim.

As they walked out of town, Joshua tugged on Pa's sleeve. "Where do we find gold?" asked Joshua. It seemed that everywhere he looked, miners were already at work. Dust-covered men, most with long beards and floppy hats, knelt by the river.

"What are they doing?" asked Joshua.

"They're panning for gold," Pa explained.

Joshua watched as the men shoveled a big pile of sand and gravel from the riverbed into a large, shallow pan. Then they added just a little water. The miners then shook the pan, letting the water wash the sand away over the edge of the pan. All the while, they watched with the eyes of a hawk for a flash of gold. Only lucky miners found gold nuggets or dust in the bottom of their pans.

At first, Joshua's family had a lot to do. Pa rented a little cabin, and Ma did her best to make it seem like home. They staked a claim by setting their picks and shovels into an empty spot by the river.

Joshua was unhappy. "There aren't any kids to play with," he grumbled. There were only a few children in the camp, and none of the boys were Joshua's age.

"If you promise not to get underfoot, you can come with me and work on the claim," Pa said.

Joshua ran to get his shovel, bucket, and pan. At the claim, Pa told Joshua to dig up a square of land next to the river. That's how Joshua learned that gold was not just in the riverbed, but in the land all through the hills. Joshua carefully dug up the dirt. Then he put the dirt in a pan and poured water from his bucket to cleanse it. This was long, slow work, and by the end of the day, Joshua didn't find anything but a spoonful of yellow specks. But the specks were gold.

Joshua often went with his father to the claim. Day after day, he worked digging up the dirt in hopes of finding gold. The day finally came when he found a nugget! It wasn't very large, just a bit larger than the head of a pin, but Joshua was happy.

"What are you going to do with it?" Pa asked.

Joshua thought for a moment and then reached out his hand. "It's for the family," he said.

"That is awfully grown-up of you, Joshua, but you keep the gold," said Pa.

That night, Joshua put the gold in his box of most precious treasures.

CHAPTER 5:
MOVING TO SACRAMENTO

Pa decided that their next stop would be Sacramento. One day in late November, the family set out once again for a new home, and that afternoon they arrived in Sacramento. "Oh, my!" cried Ma. "I forgot how nice a town could be." The town was bustling with activity. Wagons carried lumber, shovels, and large sacks of grain. Couples walked arm in arm along the wooden sidewalks.

Being in Sacramento was quite a change from Weaverville. Bakeries, blacksmiths, hotels, and

November 18, 1849: Pa and Ma have decided it's time to move from Weaverville. Susannah and I miss having friends. Ma says she's tired of living in such a dirty town. Last week, a lot of people were sick with fever. Pa hasn't found much gold here.

restaurants lined the street. Sacramento even had its own theater! Off the smaller streets that led away from Front Street, Joshua could see new wooden houses. Only here and there were people still living in tents.

"Pa, can we get down and walk around?" asked Susannah.

Pa considered it for a moment. "I don't see why not. Let's go explore our new home." He pulled the wagon over and the whole family stepped down onto the streets of Sacramento.

It seemed that their new home had something for everyone. Susannah got a tea set and held a party for her dolls. Pa eyed some shiny new tools at the dry goods store, and Ma couldn't stop looking at a bonnet with bright blue ribbon adorning it. Joshua was sure he would soon find friends.

Ma and Pa found a place to stay on the second floor of a wooden house. The family settled into their new home. Joshua and Susannah started going to school. Ma was making plans for the garden she would plant in the spring. Pa went out to the American River each day to pan for gold. Nothing could dampen their excitement—not even the rains of December, which poured down and turned the streets into mud.

In January, a heavy storm hit. Joshua went outside to watch rain pour down in sheets. He was relieved to see Pa return home.

"The rivers are overflowing," Pa said. "They were already swollen from last month's rains. Then this big storm comes. Now the river water has nowhere to go but over the banks. But we do. Let's get inside. Your ma will be worried."

When the rains finally ended and the floodwaters ebbed back into the riverbeds, most of Sacramento had been washed away. Ma and Pa decided to return to San Francisco. They used the last of their money to buy a little house. "Good," Ma sighed. "This means we're here to stay."

CHAPTER 6:
SETTLING IN SAN FRANCISCO

Pa started a construction business in San Francisco. "More and more people are moving to the city," he said. He started his new work with the good spirit he had put into gold mining. He did so well that soon he hired several workers to help him.

That fall, Joshua's family gathered with the rest of San Francisco for a happy event. California became the thirty-first state. They strolled through the streets, cheering and tooting horns.

February 1, 1850: We've moved again. Pa gave up looking for gold. We're back in San Francisco. Ma says we have moved more in the past year than she ever did in her whole life.

A year after they moved to San Francisco, Pa came home holding up a newspaper. The headline read, "Gold found in Australia!"

"What do you think?" Pa asked. "Should we go to Australia? We could make our fortune in gold!"

Joshua, Ma, and Susannah looked at Pa with alarm. But then a smile broke across his face, and the whole family burst into laughter.

From Beginning to End

James Marshall made the discovery that started the California Gold Rush. In 1848, Marshall found pea-sized lumps of gold in the American River. Word spread quickly. By the winter of 1848, the news reached the east coast of the United States and even countries around the world.

Thousands of Americans and people from other countries flocked to the goldfields. They were willing to suffer the long, dangerous journey in hopes of striking it rich. Many people traveled along the California Trail. Other people sailed around the tip of South America and then north to San Francisco. By 1853, about 330,000 people had traveled to California. Few of these people found their fortunes, but many stayed and started new lives.

Today, people can still visit the California Trail through the many books and Web sites that explore this journey. Many families have even joined a wagon train along the trail. They re-create the journey by dressing like the early pioneers. They cook over open campfires and use only pioneer's tools.